MW00639648

The
Slow Birding
Journal

The Slow Birding Journal

A Field Diary for Watching Birds Wherever You Are

Joan E. Strassmann

Illustrations by Anthony Bartley

A TarcherPerigee Book

tarcherperigee

an imprint of Penguin Random House LLC
penguinrandomhouse.com

Copyright © 2024 by Joan E. Strassmann
Penguin Random House supports copyright. Copyright fuels creativity, encourages diverse voices, promotes free speech, and creates a vibrant culture. Thank you for buying an authorized edition of this book and for complying with copyright laws by not reproducing, scanning, or distributing any part of it in any form without permission. You are supporting writers and allowing Penguin Random House to continue to publish books for every reader. Please note that no part of this book may be used or reproduced in any manner for the purpose of training artificial intelligence technologies or systems.

TarcherPerigee with tp colophon is a registered trademark of Penguin Random House LLC.

Most TarcherPerigee books are available at special quantity discounts for bulk purchase for sales promotions, premiums, fundraising, and educational needs. Special books or book excerpts also can be created to fit specific needs. For details, write: SpecialMarkets@penguinrandomhouse.com.

Library of Congress Control Number: 2024933136

ISBN: 9780593717042

Printed in the United States of America
1st Printing

Book design by Shannon Nicole Plunkett

Outdoor recreational activities are by their very nature potentially hazardous. All participants in such activities must assume the responsibility for their own actions and safety. If you have any health problems or medical conditions, consult with your physician before undertaking any outdoor activities. The information contained in this guidebook cannot replace sound judgment and good decision-making, which can help reduce risk exposure, nor does the scope of this book allow for disclosure of all the potential hazards and risks involved in such activities.

Learn as much as possible about the outdoor recreational activities in which you participate, prepare for the unexpected, and be cautious. The reward will be a safer and more enjoyable experience.

While the author has made every effort to provide accurate telephone numbers, internet addresses, and other contact information at the time of publication, neither the publisher nor the author assumes any responsibility for errors or for changes that occur after publication. Further, the publisher does not have any control over and does not assume any responsibility for author or third-party websites or their content.

For my children, Anna, Daniel, and Philip,
who love the natural world

Contents

Preface

The purpose of this journal is to suggest ways you might look more closely at birds. It presents the birds in my previous book, *Slow Birding*, and proposes activities to focus your observations. There are also free-form pages with poetic lines for inspiration.

Slow birding is a perspective on bird-watching that emphasizes birding thoughtfully, with attention to the details of birds' lives. Stop to watch the chickadees as they move from place to place, inspecting every crevice for an edible morsel. Look for the Cedar Waxwings when you hear their high whistle, and follow them as they forage for fruit. Take care to observe how the birds use time and space in their lives. You will be surprised at what you can discover.

The idea of slow birding was inspired by the Slow Food movement, which was sparked by the arrival of a McDonald's near the Spanish Steps in Rome in 1986. This group was called Arcigola, and Folco Portinari wrote their manifesto, published in 1987, which espoused a thoughtful, local, and delicious approach to food and embedded it in their politics.

The analogy adopted here is that there can be more to birding than checking a new bird off a list, satisfying as that can be. Just as Slow Food directs attention to a carefully prepared local meal, slow birding directs attention to the local birds right in front of us.

When we see a bird, a first step might be to identify it. That isn't always simple. In addition to how it looks, we can also use its behavior. But even if we can identify a bird easily, we can get so much more out of watching a bird for a while, essentially becoming one with it.

I might want to know nature better, but how can I see what I do not already know? Will I even recognize something new? How can I become a better observer? I know that I should stay still and watch, that I should take notes, but beyond that? The purpose of this little book is to give us a place to record our observations and to provide some suggestions of what is worth discovering.

For example, one might see an American Robin that hops a few steps and cocks its head. What is it doing? A Blue Jay calls from a spruce tree, then flies off to join another. What will it do next? The trilling song of a House Wren comes from deep in a bush. Is that a male waiting for a female? You can enrich your bird experiences by knowing what questions to ask, slowing down, and watching. Slow birders develop the patience and take the time to delve into the private lives of birds.

Feel free to use this journal in any order. Read about one bird or another. As with life, birding need not be linear.

How to Use This Journal

This journal is made for both written observation and sketching. Drawing can be a fruitful way to observe and capture the birds you see. You may sketch a bird as it appears before you or draw from a photograph. Either way, the act of drawing will help you focus your gaze. It will help you see more carefully. How exactly does a white circle of feathers surround the eye—as a full circle or an interrupted one? Where do the stripes along the chest end? Look carefully and capture what you see with your pencil.

It can be hard to know what to look for when you watch a bird, so this is a place of inspiration. For the sixteen birds covered in *The Slow Birding Journal*, there are specific prompts to use as you draw and write. There are also more general pages with prompts designed to inspire. The phrases are purposely short with the goal of opening your imagination. Use them as you will for watching the birds right before you. Find a comfortable seat and prepare to spend some time outside recording what you see.

Essential and Useful Apps

It is a wonderful time to be curious about the natural world. In addition to using binoculars and this journal, you can add to your experience with a few apps.

Begin with Merlin Bird ID, a free app from the Cornell Lab of Ornithology. Set it for the current season and locality, and then you can use it in two main ways. One is to answer questions about a bird you see. You can input size, color, and the like, and then Merlin will give you some possibilities. See which one looks most like your bird. This is especially useful for beginners unsure of what kind of bird they are seeing.

The most mesmerizing way to use Merlin is to put it on "Sound ID" and let it tell you what bird it hears. It will pick up the Blue Jay you hear clearly, but it will also pick up the chirps of a Song Sparrow or a Northern Cardinal. At my recent family reunion in Anacortes, Washington, it taught me how to tell the Black-capped Chickadees that I know from the Chestnut-backed Chickadees that are so common there. Merlin revolutionizes birding by ear since you can listen to what Merlin names and then learn it yourself. Remember that Merlin sometimes makes mistakes, so use it to learn the songs and calls for yourself. But as a tool to discover what is around you, it is simply superb, and for me it has transformed bird recognition, particularly in new places. It can also help you know when something you have not seen is nearby—something you might want to track down.

Maybe I should have mentioned field guides first, because these are still essential. Some people prefer a physical guide on paper, and many others use guides on their smartphones. I like both, the phone guides for in the field and the paper ones to browse at home. On my smartphone I have eBird, iBird Pro, Sibley Birds, and the Audubon Bird Guide, and whatever I can find for other countries. In book form, I have several of David Allen Sibley's books such as *The Sibley Guide to Birds*, Jon L. Dunn and Jonathan Alderfer's *Field Guide to the Birds of North America*, and Kenn Kaufman's *Kaufman Field Guide to Birds of North America*. There are books for specific groups like warblers, shorebirds, or raptors, and for specific places (see Clark and Wheeler, 2001 and Dunn and Garrett, 1997 in the Useful References section).

When you get comfortable with identifying a dozen or so local birds, you might start using eBird to record your observations. This app is also produced by the Cornell Lab of Ornithology. I love it because it not only lets me organize my bird observations but also shares them with scientists who can analyze the data compiled from millions of bird-watchers. I use the mobile version on my smartphone, entering the birds as I see them. I used to write down the birds and enter them into the computer version of the program afterward. I also entered historic data from past bird observations.

There are lots of tutorials on how to use eBird. I like to use it every day on walks of at least fifteen minutes. I keep track of the time, the place, and whether or not I recorded every bird I could or just a few. The eBird team prefers you record kinds and numbers of all the birds you can identify, and I always do that, including the House Sparrows and European Starlings, along with the rest. There are places for comments, and I try to use them a lot. On the checklist comments, I put the temperature and the weather—sunny or cloudy, mostly. It is also possible to upload photographs and sound recordings of the birds you see and hear to eBird.

If you go somewhere and take multiple bird walks, you can amalgamate them into a trip report, so you can have a list of all the birds of the trip. There is also a place to write a trip narrative, which I like to do. You can make it public or private.

I love eBird because I like to feel I'm helping the researchers understand national and global patterns of where the birds are. But I also like the way it helps me keep my bird observations organized. It tells me where I have been and what I have seen.

There is another pair of apps I use mostly for plants and insects, but they can work for birds too. They are Seek and iNaturalist. I open Seek and let it tell me what plant or insect is in the smartphone's screen, and then I upload the information to iNaturalist, which shares the data with researchers. I use them less for birds, since I don't have pictures adequate for identification in my smartphone view.

While these apps greatly improve one's ability to identify birds, it is also good to find some experts and join your local birding groups for bird walks in your area.

The
Slow Birding
Journal

PLACE

The most important thing is where you are right now. A location's beauty may vary, from your suburban backyard to the glorious dunes of Lake Michigan or the San Juan Islands in Washington State. But bring the scale down to that of one bird and a birch tree can be the universe. The closer to home you bring your gaze, the more in tune with local birds you may be and the more satisfying home can be.

The world is full of exotic places, but you do not need to go to any of them to find fascinating birds. You may not be at Thoreau's cabin, or in the Fens in England's East Anglia region, or in Valladolid, Mexico, or on the African Serengeti Plain (to name a few places Facebook friends might be extolling), but it does not matter. Nature can be found everywhere.

Look at the purslane growing between the bricks of your front porch and treasure it. Think of the woodpeckers, starlings, grackles, and chickadees coming to a feeder. These do not migrate much, which makes the willows, spruces, maples, and black walnuts in your yards and parks crucial parts of their whole world. What if they were as crucial to ours?

It should not be hard to love where you are right now. It just takes a little bit of a different perspective, one that focuses on the details that might otherwise go overlooked. I hope these activities help.

FIVE
HOME
ACTIVITIES

Window.
Let one window frame your view and draw every plant you can see. Go outside and see how many of those plants you can identify using Seek or iNaturalist. Write about what you discover.

Place: _____

Time: _____   Date: _____

Temperature: _____   Weather: _____

Plant.

Choose one plant and look at it carefully, as if you were a bird. What might it offer—food, insects or berries, nesting fluff or lichen, a place for a nest? Describe it.

Place: _____

Time: _____   Date: _____

Temperature: _____   Weather: _____

Soil.
Soil. The plants on which birds depend themselves depend on soil. Reach into the soil and let it run through your fingers if it is sandy, or roll it into a ball if it is clayey. Do this at a few other places in the meadow or forest. What is the soil like? Do you find ants in it?

Place: _____

Time: _____   Date: _____

Temperature: _____   Weather: _____

String circle. Take a piece of string and tie it into a circle. Place it on the ground and count the plants in the circle. How many different kinds do you have? Draw some of them. Move the circle a few feet away and repeat. Are there different numbers or kinds of plants there? Repeat and marvel at the diversity magnified by your simple circle.

Place: _____

Time: _____   Date: _____

Temperature: _____   Weather: _____

Gaps.
Lie on the ground in a forest or under some bushes and look up through the leaves. Draw the spaces that are left between the leaves, considering how the spaces take different shapes according to the arrangement of the leaves.

Place: _____

Time: _____   Date: _____

Temperature: _____   Weather: _____

SIXTEEN COMMON BIRDS

Blue Jay

Cyanocitta cristata

Blue Jays are gorgeous, with their jaunty crest and bright blues intensifying to near purple and a cerulean that puts the Cerulean Warbler to shame. Blue Jays love acorns. They eat them, carry them, or hide them for winter recovery when food is not so available. Think of acorns as a Blue Jay might, and sort the solid from the weevil-infested. Pick up an acorn nestled among fallen leaves on an autumn walk. An acorn might still have its cap on, making it look like something a child might design for a fairy garden. Acorns simply plop down from oak trees. Unlike maple seeds, they have no wings to spin even a few feet away from their mother tree.

Blue Jays spend a lot of time manipulating acorns, sizing them up for quality, removing their caps, and hiding them far from the original oak trees. They prefer to cache acorns when other Blue Jays are not watching. Blue Jays are very good at remembering where they have hidden their acorns.

Blue Jays are quite social, calling frequently to one another. It is worth following their calls and seeing if you can discover a roosting owl deep in a spruce. If not an owl, the Blue Jays might have discovered a Cooper's Hawk or even a feral cat.

Listen. Blue Jays have many different calls. See how many sounds you can record and describe. Count how often they make each sound. Record the sounds using Merlin and sketch the sonogram.

Place: _____

Time: _____   Date: _____

Temperature: _____   Weather: _____

Follow. Blue Jays often mob hawks and owls and pester them until they fly away. See if you can follow mobbing Blue Jays and find what they are after. If you cannot see the predator, draw the place it is likely to be hidden.

Place: _____

Time: _____   Date: _____

Temperature: _____   Weather: _____

Acorns.
Pick up a handful of acorns under an oak. If you were a Blue Jay, how many would you have selected for caching? Can you tell those with weevils from those that are sound? An acorn infested with weevils will be lighter and will have at least one small hole. You can break them open to see the weevils. How difficult is it to get that cap off for easy carrying? Can you cache a few acorns yourself, burying them in the ground or hiding them under a few leaves? Have you noticed any oak seedlings far enough from an oak tree that they must have been moved there, perhaps by a Blue Jay?

Place: _____

Time: _____   Date: _____

Temperature: _____   Weather: _____

American Robin

Turdus migratorius

If ever there is a bird for everyone, it is the American Robin. They are colorful, ever present, and often on the ground where even toddlers can see them. Feel glad when you see a robin, whether it be a brave one in the city or a timid one fleeing your approach. It feels like robins are there for us, there to remind us what a bird really is. American Robins can be found all over the country most of the year, though the birds we see in summer are probably not the same ones we encounter in winter, for they do migrate a little. Among eBirders, American Robins are the third most encountered bird, after Mourning Doves and Northern Cardinals.

Robins like our city yards and small parks because they hunt for earthworms best in fields of short grass. Those worms are important to robins to feed to their young, so robins don't even start nesting until the humidity is high enough to bring the earthworms close to the surface. But they are still under the surface, so how do the robins figure out where to peck? It turns out that they are listening for worms when they tilt their heads to the side.

But worms are mostly for babies, not adults. What the adults live on is fruit. If you see a fruit tree of some sort in the fall, you will often find American Robins and Cedar Waxwings gobbling down fruit. There are other temperate-zone birds that eat fruit, but these are the professionals.

Robins look sturdy, like the kind of bird a child would draw. Their upright stance on the ground makes them look fat, but that is just their feathers. No bird can be fat and still fly. Males and females look nearly the same, but a careful eye will tell them apart. The colors on a male are simply stronger than those on the female. This is most obvious on the heads, which are much darker black on males than on females. Juveniles are easily distinguished by their camouflage: brown flecks on an oranging breast.

Robins nest low, so it is not hard to find their nests in spring. Robin eggs are blue, ranging from the deep turquoise of a tropical sea to the pale blue of a dawning sky. They are the eggshell most often seen on the sidewalk under a nest.

Who would have thought that this commonest of all birds is so interesting? Of all the birds in this book, this might be the easiest to get out and watch! I see American Robins nearly every single day no matter which of my nearby places I visit.

Nest. See if you can find an active robin's nest. They tend to be ten to twenty feet high and out on a limb. It is not hard to follow a parent to its nest by watching. Try to watch the nest for a few minutes every day, remembering to stay far enough away that the robins are not troubled. How often does a parent visit the nest? Can you tell if it is the male or the female? If there are eggs in the nest, the female will warm them and the male will bring her food.

Place: _____

Time: _____   Date: _____

Temperature: _____   Weather: _____

Worms. Watch a robin on the ground hunting worms. How many hops do they take between stabs into the soil? Do they look with their left eye and ear or their right? How often are they successful when they stab into the ground? Count.

Place: _____

Time: _____   Date: _____

Temperature: _____   Weather: _____

Escape. How close can you get to a robin before it flies away? Walk slowly toward the robin. Do this ten times with different robins. Try the same thing in the forest as on a lawn to see if they flee sooner in the forest.

Place: _____

Time: _____   Date: _____

Temperature: _____   Weather: _____

House Wren

Troglodytes aedon

House Wrens are found across more of North and South America than any other New World songbird and are anything but rare. If you saw a tiny little bird with a tail held at a right angle to its body disappearing into the brush, you probably saw a House Wren.

Since House Wrens nest in cavities, they are attracted by nest boxes. Researchers can attract House Wrens simply by putting out more nest boxes. One study put out nest boxes in groups of three and plugged the holes of two in each group until males claimed the territories with the unplugged nest boxes, never knowing the others might become available. After that, the researchers unplugged the two other boxes in half the groups of three. This meant more females could move in. It also meant that the males seemed to have "extra" boxes, making them appear of higher quality to the females. Those females rewarded their males by laying more eggs, figuring that the females could care for the extra young and that they were worth the females' extra effort.

One of the big advances in ornithology is the increased appreciation of what female birds can do. One surprising thing is that females sing, something that used to be thought true of only some female tropical birds. In House Wrens, researchers found that females sang in variable ways, with some songs short and sounding like a human squeal and others longer and more like male songs in their composition. Females sang when soliciting copulation or when males were absent. One female sang in an attempt to evict another female from a nest box. It turns out that singing females lost fewer eggs to marauding neighboring females who might come in and stab and kill the undeveloped embryos. So females sing to tell other females to stay away. The female House Wrens viewed other females as a threat, and a greater threat than the males.

House Wrens have a delicate coloring of brown feathers speckled with black. And they have attitude. They are noisy and busy, stopping at nothing to rear the best babies they can. They have two broods a year. They switch partners readily, even cheating on each other early in the season. But when there are babies in the nest, they get tended to. Mom keeps them warm when they cannot do it themselves. Hang a wren box, and for a few months of the summer, the entertainment will be constant.

Song. House Wrens can be challenging to see because they are so small and tend to hide, but learn their song and you will discover that they are everywhere. See if you can keep track of where birds in your neighborhood sing. Try to distinguish female song early in the season.

Place: _____

Time: _____   Date: _____

Temperature: _____   Weather: _____

Nest boxes.
Put out nest boxes with an opening between 1⅛ and 1½ inches in diameter that is four to six inches above the floor of the box; the floor should be about four inches square. Put the box four to ten feet high, with some vegetation nearby and some shade for the box during the hot part of the day. You could put out several nest boxes, perhaps varying location or opening size, and see which the birds prefer. Sometimes males like to present more than one nest box to a female. Then see which they like and how it differs from the others.

Place: _____

Time: _____   Date: _____

Temperature: _____   Weather: _____

Activity. Once you have a nest in your box, keep track of the activity—how often the parents come and go and what kinds of food they bring in. You might even put a camera in the nest box. Join Cornell Lab's NestWatch online and share your observations.

Place: _____

Time: _____   Date: _____

Temperature: _____   Weather: _____

Dark–eyed Junco
Junco hyemalis

When the first Dark-eyed Juncos show up, you know that winter has really come in most of the United States. They twitter and hide, flashing their white outer tail feathers as they scurry into a pine tree or under the dead grasses.

Dark-eyed Juncos branched off from Yellow-eyed Juncos, which mostly occur in Mexico, after the Last Glacial Maximum, when the glaciers of North America extended the farthest south, about twenty thousand years ago. There are different color forms of Dark-eyed Juncos across the United States. There were other splits shown in color patterns as they flew north to different places, with those flying to Oregon to breed separating from those flying to Michigan, for example.

These winter birds have a surprise for us because males and females, young birds and old birds, do not necessarily migrate to the same places. A quick think on migration might suggest that larger, older males would go the farthest and smaller, younger females the least far, but it is just the opposite. It is the females that go far, apparently because that is what it takes for them to get enough food in winter, as they have to compete with larger males.

It is fun to listen to the songs of Dark-eyed Juncos flying through the underbrush, white outer tail feathers flashing. A male's song is not necessarily original, since they often copy songs from their neighbors, though females seem to know and prefer males with original songs.

Some of the most detailed work on preen oils was done with Dark-eyed Juncos. Did you know that birds carry their own beauty oil with them at all times? When you see them working over their feathers with their beaks, they are applying this oil, which is secreted from the preen oil gland. The gland is at the base of the tail, on the top. Female Dark-eyed Juncos prefer males that have certain volatile compounds in the preen oil. It turns out that the preen oil gland's smell actually comes from bacteria that specialize in eating the oils in the preen oil gland.

Dominance.
Put some sunflower seeds on the ground in an area you can watch, maybe three feet square. Do the birds fight for seeds, with one individual displacing another? Try to keep track for ten minutes and see if there are a few birds consistently in the best positions.

Place: _____

Time: _____   Date: _____

Temperature: _____   Weather: _____

Optimization. Put out several patches of food, close to shelter or farther from shelter or even under some weeds. Do the juncos prefer the safer place? Count them at five-minute intervals.

Place: _____

Time: _____   Date: _____

Temperature: _____   Weather: _____

Grouping. Scatter sunflower seeds in a broad path several yards long. Do the juncos group to feed close to one another or spread out? Count them in different areas. Are they choosing to be close together perhaps as protection from predators?

Place: _____

Time: _____   Date: _____

Temperature: _____   Weather: _____

Northern Flicker

Colaptes auratus

There are two different colors of Northern Flickers, called yellow-shafted and red-shafted. This refers to the color under the wings and under the tail. They were once considered to be two species with a large hybrid zone just east of the Rockies and extending into British Columbia. The differences between yellow and red flickers arose during the time glaciers covered northern North America. As a result, the two kinds of flickers migrate south in winter to different sides of the Rockies.

Flickers eat mostly ants, which they hunt on the ground, flicking their beak left to right in the short grass, or probing under a rock or log. It is a wonder that this relatively large bird (among woodpeckers, only the Pileated Woodpecker is larger) can survive on these tiny and inconspicuous creatures that mostly live underground.

Because they eat ants, Northern Flickers are unusual among woodpeckers in not having a feeding territory that they defend against other flickers. This lack of competition for food makes sense because they are mostly taking worker ants or ant grubs, which are scattered and renewable resources. If you see two flickers feeding in the same lawn, you cannot assume they are in any way related. They might as well be completely unrelated people in line at the neighborhood taco truck.

Flickers chisel out their own nest cavities from the trunks of trees. Aspens are preferred not only because of their soft wood but also because they rot from the inside out, leaving a hollow core that's perfect for a flicker nest. Flickers work hard to chip out their nests, but they do not always get to keep them. Many other animals love to take over Northern Flicker cavities—including other woodpeckers, chickadees, nuthatches, bluebirds, some duck species, small hawks, owls, and even mammals like squirrels, wood rats, and weasels. Because so many other organisms depend on them, Northern Flickers are considered a keystone species. Biodiversity would plummet if flickers did not create cavities.

What exactly is it like inside a flicker nest? The average number of eggs is eight, though females can lay as many as twelve small eggs in a clutch. The eggs hatch in about eleven days. After that, there are three stages to managing their excretion. Parents eat the hatchlings' feces until the chicks are about ten days old, prodding them to defecate by poking their cloacae. Next, the parents— usually the father—pick up the hatchlings' fecal sacs and dump them far enough away so that predators cannot use the odor of the droppings to find the nest.

At about two weeks of age, the chicks rise from the nest floor and cling to the interior walls of their home. At this point, when they defecate, the feces simply fall to the bottom of the cavity, so their once-cozy nest becomes their latrine. Any hatchlings that die at this stage simply fall down there and stay. The parents sometimes help the situation by chipping off bits of wood from the cavity interior to cover up the mess underneath. After about twenty-five days, the chicks are coaxed out of their nest by their shrieking parents, who call loudly until the youngsters emerge.

. . . .

Foraging. Northern Flickers are often on the ground foraging for ants right between the concrete slabs of a sidewalk. Sit in your handy portable chair and watch exactly where they are foraging, noting how they move and how long they stay in one place.

Place: _____

Time: _____ Date: _____

Temperature: _____ Weather: _____

Nest.

Nest. Northern Flickers are common nearly everywhere in North America, so nests are not hard to find if you watch and listen for flickers and follow them in spring or early summer to a cavity in an aspen or another tree. Set up your chair a distance away and count how long it is between feedings. If it is early enough in the season, you might even see a fecal sac being carried away by a father. If you visit the nest often enough, you might witness the parents calling their flickerlings out of their safe cavity and into the world to hunt ants on their own.

Place: _____

Time: _____   Date: _____

Temperature: _____   Weather: _____

Trees.

Find some dead or dying trees in your neighborhood and list the wildlife in them. Catalog changes over time.

Place: _____

Time: _____   Date: _____

Temperature: _____   Weather: _____

Cooper's Hawk

Accipiter cooperii

If the songbirds suddenly lift up from your feeder and flee, look for a Cooper's Hawk. If you see feathers on the ground, look for a Cooper's Hawk. If you hear a hoarse, throaty call, a *ka-ka-ka* or a *whaa* or even high whistles, look for a Cooper's Hawk. This is the hawk of our times, one that has made our neighborhoods its home.

If you are lucky enough to see a pair of Cooper's Hawks together, you will notice that one bird is much bigger than the other. Unlike with most mammals, with hawks the bigger bird is the female. A female hawk's large size may help her fight other females for the right to be in a certain male's territory. Males fight one another too, however, so shouldn't they be large as well? Being smaller could be an advantage for hunting agile prey, particularly other birds. Perhaps the smaller males do more of the hunting while the larger females defend the young from racoons and other nest predators.

Cooper's Hawks mostly eat birds, but they also eat small mammals. In one study in Ithaca, New York, this consisted of twenty-four bird species and four mammal species, most commonly European Starlings, Northern Flickers, Eastern Meadowlarks, American Robins, and eastern chipmunks. Apparently it takes about sixty-six birds or mammals to raise a single chick to six weeks, not counting the food brought to the mother during the month she incubates the eggs. This is four meals a day during the first week, five a day during the second week, then varying between seven and nine a day during the remaining weeks. If you are wondering how there are any birds left when Cooper's Hawks are around, it is important to know that most of the birds they catch are the young of the year, not experienced adults.

Unlike the young of songbirds, those of Cooper's Hawks do not leave the nest area after they can fly. Instead, they hang out in the nest or on the limbs adjoining it, waiting for their parents to bring in food. After a month or two, adults will simply put whole prey near the nest for their young to grab.

Making one's living off birds has its challenges, since they can fly away so easily from a predator. But certain traits make the hunt easier. It turns out that Cooper's Hawks that hunt primarily birds have longer middle toes, presumably to snatch birds out of the sky.

It may be horrifying to see a Cooper's Hawk descend on your backyard feeder and leave with a songbird in its clutches, but remember that songbirds are even more relentless predators on insects, requiring thousands of them to rear each nestling.

. . . .

Nest.
See if you can find a Cooper's Hawk nest. They are often built near the main trunk of a tree, sometimes piled on top of old squirrels' nests, though Cooper's Hawks use fresh green twigs. Once you find a nest, watch how often the male brings in food. You might even witness a brief copulation, often performed in exchange for a starling or chipmunk.

Place: _____

Time: _____   Date: _____

Temperature: _____   Weather: _____

Plucking post. Cooper's Hawks have plucking posts
where they process their catch, usually within fifty yards of the
nest. Watch the post to see if you can witness a hawk processing
a kill there.

Place: _____

Time: _____   Date: _____

Temperature: _____   Weather: _____

Bird feeder.
If a Cooper's Hawk visits your bird feeder, see if it catches a bird. See how long it stays close to your feeder and from where it watches the feeder. Record the responses of the other birds.

Place: _____

Time: _____   Date: _____

Temperature: _____   Weather: _____

Cedar Waxwing

Bombycilla cedrorum

C edar Waxwings are beautiful birds, from the black mask
outlined in white to the feathery crest to the tail dipped in
yellow the color of yolk. Best of all are the little waxy tips
of crimson on the ends of some wing feathers. Their other colors
are more subtle, a yellow wash on the belly and chestnut on the

head and neck, fading to gray across the back and then intensifying to black on the tail.

Cedar Waxwings are fruit specialists, eating nearly nothing else. Where fruit occurs, it occurs in abundance, so Cedar Waxwings are not territorial, instead flying around in flocks looking for fruit, which can be anything from cherries and berries to the smaller fruits of mistletoe and hackberry. In any given place, Cedar Waxwings arrive unpredictably from on high, their sweet whistles in the morning sky too high-pitched for some to hear.

It takes a special physiology to live on a diet of so much fruit. In one study, blueberries took twenty-eight minutes from the time they were swallowed to the time what was left exited a waxwing's digestive system. Chokecherries took forty minutes, and black cherries took twenty minutes for the same path.

The one time Cedar Waxwings need to stay put is when they are nesting, which they do later in the year than other birds so that plenty of new fruits are available. This is also the one time they collect insects, though even the young flourish mainly on fruits after their first two days of life. At all stages of Cedar Waxwings' lives, their nests tend to be built in a kind of exploded aggregation, not clustered together yet not far apart.

At one study site on an island in Lake Erie, Cedar Waxwings nested mostly in maple, cedar, and fruit trees. The waxwings placed their nests five to twenty feet above the ground. They built their nests of grass, twigs, and plant stems, then lined the bowls with cobwebs, moss, and soft grasses. The nests were loose and bulky and had taken only five days to build, but those were busy days. Each nest contained about 2,327 pieces of plant material.

Listen. Cedar Waxwings are easiest to find by listening for the high, thin whistles they make as they fly in small flocks from one place to another. See if you can hear them, and then look for them to see what they are doing as they whistle.

Place: _____

Time: _____   Date: _____

Temperature: _____   Weather: _____

Flocks. Cedar Waxwing flocks are usually small. See if you can count the birds in a flock and watch what they do. When they land, how close together are they?

Place: _____

Time: _____   Date: _____

Temperature: _____   Weather: _____

Fruit. Find a fruit tree with Cedar Waxwings in it. How do they eat? Do they spread through the tree or clump, perhaps for safety? Can you see any differences between fruit they swallow and fruit they reject?

Place: _____

Time: _____   Date: _____

Temperature: _____   Weather: _____

European Starling

Sturnus vulgaris

Europeans Starlings are highly successful and social birds that can be found across North America, largely in edge environments where the open fields they use for foraging meet forests with trees for nest sites. They also nest frequently in human-constructed buildings and seem almost uniquely well adapted to the built environment.

They are not native to the Americas. As a member of the American Acclimatization Society, Eugene Schieffelin thought that New York City needed European birds, especially the birds of Shakespeare. In 1890 he released sixty European Starlings in Central Park. He released another forty birds in the same place in the following year. Now there are over two hundred million European Starlings in the United States. Like House Sparrows, they are at home with us, nesting in our eaves and eating our garbage. Their overlap with our own habitations may make them seem more common than they are, though they are indeed very common.

One reason for the starlings' startling success is that they seemingly eat just about anything. Starlings love insects of all kinds: snails, millipedes, and spiders. They also eat many kinds of fruits and nuts, including acorns. But what they eat is not the reason that we are concerned about them. It is that they nest in cavities that other birds, especially woodpeckers, might use. Starlings are a problem for cavity-nesting birds, but it is a problem made worse by habitat loss. However, since starlings need open areas, they are not a problem in continuous forests.

In the wintertime, starlings form spectacular murmurations of thousands of birds soaring, turning, turning again, then weaving around, only to soar as if one again. These evening rivers of life stay in constant motion but do not go anywhere, instead swirling around a roosting point on the ground to which they will all drop at sunset. In a murmuration, each starling flies smoothly by keeping track of six or seven near neighbors. With this number, the starlings can turn and bend optimally, particularly after one sights a predator.

Because starlings are highly social and are frequently found on neighborhood lawns or nesting in the eaves of houses, they are particularly easy to watch in all phases of their lives. When the young leave the nest, they are often on the ground in fields, where they run up to their parents to beg for a morsel. Once they're independent, these teenage birds form large groups where their buzzy calls can be easily heard.

Starlings are not going away, so we might as well take advantage of how easy they are to watch. Just remember how important it is not to move species around.

. . . .

Count. Sometimes it seems like European Starlings are everywhere. See if you can count them on a walk of a certain distance in your neighborhood. Try the same thing in different habitats, perhaps deeper into the city, in a city park, a farm, or a forest. Choose two or more places for each habitat so that you can account for variation within a habitat type. Where are starlings most common?

Place: _____

Time: _____   Date: _____

Temperature: _____   Weather: _____

Nest. In early spring, males will display at their nest sites to attract females. Watch their displays and listen to their vocalizations. You might also witness a fight for a cavity. What happens, and who wins?

Place: _____

Time: _____ Date: _____

Temperature: _____ Weather: _____

Vigilance. Particularly in autumn, starlings form foraging groups on the ground. Watch how individuals move. Do they go to the center of the group or away from it? Are some vigilant, with their heads up, looking around while others feed? Do they take turns?

Place: _____

Time: _____   Date: _____

Temperature: _____   Weather: _____

House Sparrow

Passer domesticus

The cheerfully monotonous cheeps of House Sparrows are among the first bird sounds a human baby usually hears, since sparrows so often nest under house eaves. They are also easy to see nearly everywhere around us, as they travel in small flocks looking for breadcrumbs or other morsels that we might drop. A House Sparrow tussle over a crust of bread is a common city sight.

House Sparrows were purposely introduced to New York from Europe and spread rapidly, following our settlements and originally feasting on the seeds in hay for horses. As horses came to be replaced by cars, sparrows declined, but they remain common in many parts of the country. Since their introduction, sparrows have displaced some native birds, particularly because sparrows do not migrate away in winter. Eastern Bluebirds and Tree Swallows are among those most likely to have suffered, since they return from their migrations after House Sparrows have already claimed nest cavities.

House Sparrows have a solution to the age-old question of how many young to raise. Since food availability is highly variable between years, it is hard to predict how many chicks the parents can rear in any given year, so they make an extra. Sparrow mothers start incubating the first eggs before the last one is laid, giving the first to hatch a head start over its later siblings. In years when food is less available, the last chick will get less than its siblings. But do the weaker, last-laid chicks actually die? It turns out that they do nearly half the time, unable to compete with their siblings when the parents cannot bring in quite enough food for all. After the spare chick dies, the parents maintain the same feeding rate, so the remaining chicks get more food and thrive.

House Sparrows are associated with the presence of humans all over the world. This is so true that if a town is abandoned, the House Sparrows also leave. This overlap with our presence makes them easy to watch. It also might make them seem like a bigger problem to native birds than they actually are. They should not have been introduced, but the harm they cause to the native birds is less than it might seem.

Transect. Take a short walk in your neighborhood and note how often you hear House Sparrows. Do the same in another neighborhood. Then compare those two samples of the House Sparrows' presence to what you find when you go to the country and listen for them there. Maybe you can find a couple of farms and a couple of nature trails. Where are the sparrows most common? Be sure to count only House Sparrows.

Place: _____

Time: _____ Date: _____

Temperature: _____ Weather: _____

Fighting.

House Sparrows very visibly fight over food. See if you can watch several fights, perhaps in a city square from a café. Toss down a few crumbs and watch the birds come. How many try to take the crumbs? Are they males or females? What happens if you put the crumbs in different places?

Place: _____

Time: _____   Date: _____

Temperature: _____   Weather: _____

Pattern.
Males have a dark brown bib that gets larger during breeding season. See if you can identify the bibs and note where and when you see males with larger bibs.

Place: _____

Time: _____   Date: _____

Temperature: _____   Weather: _____

Northern Cardinal

Cardinalis cardinalis

Male Northern Cardinals are a brilliant tomato. They have a jaunty crest and a black mask and chin flanking a bill so strong that bird banders have to use steel bands instead of the usual aluminum to prevent the birds from removing them. Female Northern Cardinals, with their tan and russet coloring, are just as beautiful, if more subtle, than the males.

Northern Cardinals like edge habitat, neither forest nor meadow. This means they are common in our gardens and yards. They are frequent visitors to bird feeders, where sunflower seeds are their particular favorite. Northern Cardinals sometimes nest in nonnative plants like Amur honeysuckle and multiflora rose, which produce red fruit to eat. Unfortunately, nests in honeysuckle and rose tend to be built much lower than nests in natural vegetation and are therefore more vulnerable to predation. Further, the red fruit of these non-native plants makes it easy for males to develop a bright red color without the effort of finding the unusual berries usually required for redness. This might seem to be a good thing for the males, but it means that color becomes less useful to the females as an indicator of quality when choosing a mate.

Listen to a Northern Cardinal sing. Its clear notes are unmistakable, and yet each bird has its own way of singing. When they are young, cardinals learn the songs of their neighbors and copy them.

Is it a surprise that female cardinals also sing? After all, they are apparently the ones to choose their mate, so they shouldn't have to sing to attract one. But song is their voice, and once they are mated, singing can tell the male when to bring in food. Males sing or give *chip* calls, much simpler and shorter sounds that resemble the clink of china. During the nesting period, if a female sang after an approaching male gave *chip* calls, the male was more likely to come to the nest than if she remained silent. If the male's initial vocalizations included song, it seemed that the female could give two different signals. If she sang songs made up of different syllable types than the male's, the male was again more likely to come to the nest than if she remained silent. However, if she sang songs with syllable types that matched the male's, this seemed to be a "no, thanks" or "stay away" signal even stronger than her silence.

. . . .

Song.
See if you can get to know the individual songs of the Northern Cardinals closest to home. Look at their sonograms on Merlin and draw the patterns of several different birds in your neighborhood.

Place: _____

Time: _____   Date: _____

Temperature: _____   Weather: _____

Feeders.
Put out several feeders with different kinds of seeds and see what the cardinals prefer. Count their visits to different feeders. See if they go together or separately to the feeders.

Place: _____

Time: _____   Date: _____

Temperature: _____   Weather: _____

Rural. Go into the countryside and find a place to watch cardinals. See if you can hear differences in their songs from those of the city birds.

Place: _____

Time: _____   Date: _____

Temperature: _____   Weather: _____

Northern Mockingbird

Mimus polyglottos

Northern Mockingbirds sing a lot, forage on our lawns, and are common, at least in Texas and the Southeast. There, one territory abuts another, making territory boundary disputes easy to spot. The birds dance along an invisible line, hopping vigorously and sometimes flying up in the air against one another. Males generally fight males, and females generally fight females.

Mockingbird territories need to contain open areas for foraging, trees or shrubs for nesting, and shrubs for sheltering fledglings. The mix of open and bush is what makes human environments attractive to mockingbirds and brings them to our neighborhoods, where they often stay all year long.

Once males have established their territories, they sing to attract females. A mockingbird's song lifts into the air, notes following one another in a melody Mozart might envy. Mockingbirds can go on and on, ever varying in their performance. Their songs repeat and change and always build on what went before, like in a Philip Glass piece. Their songs come from melodies in the environment, particularly those they hear when they are young. They copy the songs of other birds like Carolina Wrens, Tufted Titmice, Northern Cardinals, and Blue Jays and even sounds of other animals like frogs and toads.

Mockingbirds sing higher-pitched songs in areas with lots of human traffic. Artificial noises—the sound of automobiles driving down the highway, the low grinding of garbage trucks, the hum of air conditioners—tend to be low frequency. If a mockingbird male wants to attract a female or defend his territory, he must sing in a way that distinguishes his song from the background noise.

Besides singing, Northern Mockingbirds spend a lot of time foraging, often on the ground looking for insects. Sometimes foraging mockingbirds quickly open and shut their wings, flashing white wing patches, which may startle insects, making them easier to catch.

Mockingbirds are smart. They can tell one human from another, and they particularly scold anyone approaching anywhere close to a nest. If the same person approaches more than once, mockingbirds will notice the person from a greater distance, though they can be fooled if the person wears different hats.

. . . .

Song. Listen to a Northern Mockingbird sing. See if you can find a way to draw the song, perhaps looking at the sonogram Merlin produces. Can you count how many phrases are repeated or if there are any repeated sounds? Compare mockingbird song among individuals and in different places. See if you can identify anything a mockingbird is imitating.

Place: _____

Time: _____   Date: _____

Temperature: _____   Weather: _____

Foraging.
See if you can follow a Northern Mockingbird for five minutes, recording everything it does. As it forages, how far apart are its hops on the ground? Does it flash the white spots in its wings before moving on?

Place: _____

Time: _____ Date: _____

Temperature: _____ Weather: _____

Territoriality. Get a sense for which mockingbirds are where. See if you can find a territorial boundary and watch mockingbirds fighting over it. See if your local mockingbirds sing from the same perches regularly.

Place: _____

Time: _____   Date: _____

Temperature: _____   Weather: _____

Yellow-rumped Warbler

Setophaga coronata

Yellow-rumped Warblers are so common, particularly in winter, that to some people they do not bring joy but are checked off as simply another "butter butt." Others cherish even these common warblers, marveling at them as they hunt for insects, flying out quickly and then returning to their perch. They are so colorful and nicely patterned that we are lucky they are common.

Yellow-rumped Warblers can be split into two well-known subspecies called the Audubon Warbler and Myrtle Warbler. Both have the characteristic yellow rumps, but the western Audubon's Warblers have yellow throats, whereas the eastern Myrtle Warblers have white. The two subspecies are known to interbreed in central Canada, where their ranges overlap—in these hybrid zones, birds with mixed characteristics can be seen. Though hybrids make it complicated, many experts think that the two warblers should be viewed as entirely different species.

Yellow-rumped Warblers breed in the north, dipping down into New England, northern Michigan, and the Rockies and Sierras. They nest in conifers both deep in forests and on edges and winter in edge habitats and brush such as willow, bayberry, and juniper thickets.

Yellow-rumped Warblers are famous for being able to digest wax using high levels of bile acids, something few other birds can do. Having access to this extra food source allows them to stay farther north in winter than other species.

Yellow-rumped Warblers were the subject of one of the most famous ecological studies of all time, which explored how different species managed to coexist in the same areas despite competing for the same resources. It turned out that though different warbler species foraged in the same trees, they actually specialized on insects from different parts of the tree. By splitting their focus to different parts of the tree, a variety of species could coexist. Yellow-rumped Warblers used the broadest swath of the tree, from top to bottom, from close to the trunk to the tenderest branch tips. They were the only species that spent time in the bottom ten feet of the tree, though they could also be found at the very top and in intermediate zones.

Foraging.

Watch a Yellow-rumped Warbler forage for five or more minutes. Is it moving through the vegetation or flying out from a perch to catch insects? Can you see what it catches? Are other species foraging nearby? If it is foraging in a tree, see if you can determine what area of the tree it is using. Try recording your observations by talking into your smartphone instead of writing.

Place: _____

Time: _____ Date: _____

Temperature: _____ Weather: _____

Interacting. Yellow-rumped Warblers are so common,

particularly in places they winter, that you might be able to
see them interacting. Do they displace each other on favored
hunting perches? How else do they interact?

Place: _____

Time: _____ Date: _____

Temperature: _____ Weather: _____

Nest.

Watch a nest in spring if the warblers occur in your area. See how often the parents feed the babies. See if there is one young bird that is much larger than the others, which might be a cowbird. Remember, it is illegal to interfere with breeding birds, even cowbirds, so do not remove it from the nest.

Place: _____

Time: _____ Date: _____

Temperature: _____ Weather: _____

White–throated
Sparrow

Zonotrichia albicollis

Both male and female White-throated Sparrows come in two different varieties. One has a white stripe over the eye and a thin black line heading back from the eye, while the other has a tan stripe over the eye and a russet line heading back from the eye. The birds with white stripes usually cannot produce offspring by mating with each other, so they prefer to mate with tan-striped birds instead. White-striped males are more aggressive than tan-striped males and more likely to mate outside the pair bond. The color differences are most pronounced in the breeding season.

In the winter, White-throated Sparrows show dominance interactions at feeders, often fighting for seeds on the ground below a feeder. Dominance interactions are easy to see: If one bird moves to a spot and the bird that was there moves away, the first bird is dominant to the second one. If one is eating and raises its feathers or wings when another approaches and the newcomer leaves, that is dominance. If one lunges at another, that is dominance.

White-throated Sparrows prefer to eat seeds in the company of other birds. More than that, they prefer safe places close to vegetation or far from human dwellings. Seeds under vegetation may be the most preferred of all.

The song of the White-throated Sparrow is nearly as haunting as the loon's and is easily remembered by the words "Pure, sweet Canada, Canada, Canada." There is an interesting change in the song that appeared only recently in Alberta, Canada. The birds shortened "Canada" to simply "Cana," making it "Pure, sweet Cana, Cana, Cana." This song variation has now appeared in the east, presumably learned on wintering grounds, so now it should be listened for anywhere.

Pattern. Look carefully at White-throated Sparrows to see if you can distinguish the white ones from the tan ones. Males do not look different than females, so white or tan could be either sex. Count the numbers of the two patterns.

Place: _____

Time: _____   Date: _____

Temperature: _____   Weather: _____

Dominance. Put some seeds on the ground in different places, denser and less dense, close and far from vegetation. See which place the birds prefer. See if they fight over the best places with one displacing another. See if white-striped birds displace tan-striped birds at the best places.

Place: _____

Time: _____ Date: _____

Temperature: _____ Weather: _____

Song.
Listen carefully to the birds in your area. What song are they singing? See if you can hear any variations in the standard "Pure, sweet Canada, Canada, Canada."

Place: _____

Time: _____   Date: _____

Temperature: _____   Weather: _____

American Coot

Fulica americana

American Coots have plump black bodies, white beaks, and vivid green legs. They seem to be in almost every lake, marsh, or impoundment. Unlike most water birds, they do not have webbed feet. Instead, their toes have been shaped for water life and have evolved phalanxes that fold going forward and spread when pushed backward, just what a swimmer needs.

Coots eat vegetation above water, under water, and even on land. They are usually in groups where their numbers help protect individuals from predation, both because they can take turns being alert and because it makes any one bird less likely to be eaten. Groups are highly variable in size.

In the spring, coots pair up and fight to defend a bit of marsh or lake that has the reedy growth they need for nests. Acquiring and defending that territory is likely to involve lots of drama— fights, running across the water at each other, and much calling. But once they have the territory, the parents build a simple nest of dead reeds. The female lays an egg every day or two in the nest. After the first one or two eggs have been laid, both parents take turns incubating the eggs, which ultimately number between eight and twelve.

Female coots frequently lay eggs in the nests of other coots, who then struggle to recognize which are their own chicks and which are not. Chicks with very bright red heads garner the most parental attention. Since the first-laid eggs are more likely to be their own, coot parents care less for later-born chicks.

By the time the last egg in a coot nest hatches, some chicks will already be out of the nest, bobbing up and down in the water among the reeds, peeping incessantly for food, and thrusting their gaudy heads at their parents. These little chicks are precocious, capable of getting about by themselves as soon as their feathers dry after hatching, but they depend on the food their parents give them for at least a month. Knowing which chicks to feed and when is a life-or-death question in the coot world. The system seems complicated, but the commonness of coots attests that it must work.

Groups. How many American Coots are in a group?
See if you can count several groups. Do coots ever move from
one group to another? Are groups of different sizes on lakes of
different sizes?

Place: _____

Time: _____ Date: _____

Temperature: _____ Weather: _____

Chicks.
See if you can find breeding coots with their redheaded young. They will be secretive in the reeds, so be still. Watch a chick for as long as you can and see how often a parent feeds it and what else it does. Watch a parent and see how many chicks it feeds.

Place: _____

Time: _____   Date: _____

Temperature: _____   Weather: _____

Predators.

If you live in an area with visible predators like alligators, see how big the groups of American Coots are both close to and far from the predators.

Place: _____

Time: _____ Date: _____

Temperature: _____ Weather: _____

Great Egret

Ardea alba

Humans nearly drove the Great Egret to extinction by collecting its feathers for hats. Strong efforts by many, including a group of women eschewing hat feathers and fighting for the birds, finally saved this species, and many other people developed a new perspective on conservation.

The Great Egret is a bird of the wetlands, salt and fresh, large and small. A Great Egret stands tall, white, and thin, patiently waiting for fish and other prey to swim near enough to catch or probing for crustaceans like crayfish. Often they are alone, but dozens can aggregate in particularly rich waters.

Great Egrets build their nests in dense groups called rookeries. Rookeries often form in trees in a swamp or on a small island, where they are difficult for predators like foxes or coyotes to reach. Nests in the center of the colony get even more protection than that provided by the island itself.

Living in dense rookeries is possible only because the nesting adults can fly far from them in search of food for their young. Where to nest and where to eat is a trade-off Great Egrets do not necessarily have to make, but the fish that they depend on are not a predictable resource. Some years fish will be much more plentiful than others. Mothers will lay more eggs than they are likely to be able to see to adulthood, hoping for plenty of food so that they can rear all the chicks. In years when fish are less abundant, however, they have evolved a way to jettison just one chick without starving all of them using a system that takes the choice out of the parent's beaks. Unlike most birds, Great Egrets begin to incubate their eggs immediately after the first one is laid. The last Great Egret egg will hatch when the chick from the first-laid egg is already two to four days old, making it no match for its older siblings in the competition for food.

Groups. How many Great Egrets are foraging together in the water? Do those near the edge of the group catch more fish? Do they juggle their positions in the group?

Place: _____

Time: _____ Date: _____

Temperature: _____ Weather: _____

Rookery. Find a rookery of Great Egrets during breeding season. Are the nests at the same stage in the breeding cycle, and if not, are edge nests younger than more central ones? Are Great Egret nests clumped or dispersed among nests of other species?

Place: _____

Time: _____   Date: _____

Temperature: _____   Weather: _____

Competition. Watch a nest with chicks in it. How do they interact? Does it change when a parent comes in, and if so, how? Is there a dominance hierarchy?

Place: _____

Time: _____   Date: _____

Temperature: _____   Weather: _____

Snow Goose
Anser caerulescens

A Snow Goose on land is an unassuming bird, white with a mostly pink bill and pink legs. Its dark eye is unadorned on an otherwise white head, giving it a friendly and innocent look. The white head is sometimes stained orange-brown from grubbing for food in iron-rich mud. Its wingtips are dipped in black. Another form, once called the Blue Goose, is dark blue-gray except for the white head.

Snow Geese spend the winter in southern marshes, where young males and females pair up. In late winter they fly north again, the male Snow Goose following his partner to her breeding ground and forsaking his natal ground and his family.

A Snow Goose first sees the world when she pecks her way out of an egg near the ocean's edge in the high Arctic. She is usually one of five chicks in the nest. The nest is soft from downy feathers from the mother's own breast and warm from the mother's body. If the chick hatches from the first or last egg her mother lays, she will start out smaller, since these eggs are smaller, but the chick catches up to her siblings very quickly. Surprisingly, some chicks are unrelated to the mother that warms them, the result of egg dumping by a female who sneaks an egg into another's nest. By six weeks the young can fly, just in time for the long flight south. They will leave behind a nesting ground that may well be nearly destroyed by the huge population of Snow Geese.

During winter, Snow Geese grub for plant roots but also discover rice, an abundant foreign delicacy that has caused their population to explode. Snow Geese find comfort and safety in numbers. They nest and migrate in large groups, in which diseases like avian cholera can be easily transmitted from bird to bird. The risk of disease must be weighed against the threat posed by predators like Arctic foxes and Herring Gulls. The Snow Geese nesting most centrally on their breeding grounds suffer less predation because the predators approach the group from one side or another.

Disease, crowding, habitat destruction, and death are part of the Snow Goose world, yet still they inspire as they ineluctably fly north for another short breeding summer at the top of our planet.

Flight. Watch Snow Geese flying overhead. How many are in each arm of the V formation? Do they change position? Can you see the much smaller Ross's Geese mixed in?

Place: _____

Time: _____   Date: _____

Temperature: _____   Weather: _____

Foraging. Watch Snow Geese foraging. What do they eat? What size groups are they in? Are some vigilant while others eat? Compare this at two or more locations.

Place: _____

Time: _____   Date: _____

Temperature: _____   Weather: _____

Blue. See if you can spot some blue geese. Are they mixed in with the white ones? Can you detect family pairings of blue and white forms?

Place: _____

Time: _____   Date: _____

Temperature: _____   Weather: _____

MUSE,
FREE–FORM
OBSERVATIONS

Willow leaves quivered like rain against their drooping yellow branches.

Bird: _____

Place: _____

Time: _____   Date: _____

Temperature: _____   Weather: _____

*Black Skimmers sliced their lower beaks through
the bay waters, hoping for fish.*

Bird: _____

Place: _____

Time: _____   Date: _____

Temperature: _____   Weather: _____

Bubbles pimple the sand as the waves recede,
promising hidden food for shorebirds.

Bird: _____

Place: _____

Time: _____   Date: _____

Temperature: _____   Weather: _____

Crows fly west, far from their undiscovered roost.

Bird: _____

Place: _____

Time: _____   Date: _____

Temperature: _____   Weather: _____

As still as an American Bittern, I watched by the marsh.

Bird: _____

Place: _____

Time: _____ Date: _____

Temperature: _____ Weather: _____

*Their white-edged beaks showed above the muddy nest edge—
nestlings about to fledge.*

Bird: _____

Place: _____

Time: _____   Date: _____

Temperature: _____   Weather: _____

How many greens can I see in the forest?
How many birds can I hear?

Bird: _____

Place: _____

Time: _____   Date: _____

Temperature: _____   Weather: _____

*Treasure the first Chimney Swift of spring
and the last hummingbird of fall.*

Bird: _____

Place: _____

Time: _____   Date: _____

Temperature: _____   Weather: _____

Gulls circle noisily, finding fleeting treasure in our waste.

Bird: _____

Place: _____

Time: _____   Date: _____

Temperature: _____   Weather: _____

Brown-eyed Susans fade as the asters come into their own.
The bumble bees are heavy with pollen.

Bird: _____

Place: _____

Time: _____   Date: _____

Temperature: _____   Weather: _____

What bird is that, singing over and over?

Bird: _____

Place: _____

Time: _____ Date: _____

Temperature: _____ Weather: _____

A Downy Woodpecker exclaimed from the largest tree in the smallest city park.

Bird: _____

Place: _____

Time: _____   Date: _____

Temperature: _____   Weather: _____

Cedars line the stream while the hemlocks have mostly collapsed into the water, blocking my kayak.

Bird: _____

Place: _____

Time: _____   Date: _____

Temperature: _____   Weather: _____

A Snowy Egret walks under the rookery,
lifting its yellow feet high.

Bird: _____

Place: _____

Time: _____   Date: _____

Temperature: _____   Weather: _____

Borders are my favorite, whether between prairie and forest, marsh and wood, or along the endless shore.

Bird: _____

Place: _____

Time: _____   Date: _____

Temperature: _____   Weather: _____

A puddle of rainwater delights.

Bird: _____

Place: _____

Time: _____   Date: _____

Temperature: _____   Weather: _____

A bird's eye and the color of its legs can help when feathers alone confuse.

Bird: _____

Place: _____

Time: _____   Date: _____

Temperature: _____   Weather: _____

*White-eyed Vireos remain while Scarlet Tanagers
and all the warblers fly north.*

Bird: _____

Place: _____

Time: _____ Date: _____

Temperature: _____ Weather: _____

*The sun does not fade after setting when a few clouds
magnify the orange light we no longer see.*

Bird: _____

Place: _____

Time: _____   Date: _____

Temperature: _____   Weather: _____

How much time can you spend doing exactly what you like?

Bird: _____

Place: _____

Time: _____   Date: _____

Temperature: _____   Weather: _____

I told my daughter a story as we walked through the forest.

Bird: _____

Place: _____

Time: _____   Date: _____

Temperature: _____   Weather: _____

Windows suffice when it is too cold to touch the branches.

Bird: _____

Place: _____

Time: _____   Date: _____

Temperature: _____   Weather: _____

*I finally remembered to bring a portable chair
into the soft meadow overlooking a lake.*

Bird: _____

Place: _____

Time: _____   Date: _____

Temperature: _____   Weather: _____

Even the pigeons look different in Venice.

Bird: _____

Place: _____

Time: _____   Date: _____

Temperature: _____   Weather: _____

194 · Muse, Free-Form Observations

Watching the birds and remembering a childhood family.

Bird: _____

Place: _____

Time: _____   Date: _____

Temperature: _____   Weather: _____

*Once I kept a bird journal, wondering at
every flash of yellow or red.*

Bird: _____

Place: _____

Time: _____   Date: _____

Temperature: _____   Weather: _____

Sit among the falling leaves in the afternoon quiet.

Bird: _____

Place: _____

Time: _____   Date: _____

Temperature: _____   Weather: _____

Acknowledgments

I thank everyone who has helped me on this birding journey. My husband, David Queller, has been my frequent companion into the forests and meadows, has taught bird classes with me, and has read everything I have written, including this journal. For this and much more, I thank him. My children, my sisters, and my parents have gone on many birding trips with me and have been an inspiration. I thank Cin-Ty Lee for marvelous field trips, bird classes taught together, and a new vision of birds. I also thank the many generations of undergraduates at Rice University who taught me to see birds with fresh eyes. For bringing this journal to life, I thank my agent, Michelle Tessler; my editor, Jacob Surpin; and the excellent team at TarcherPerigee.

Useful References

This journal follows the birds presented in *Slow Birding: The Art and Science of Enjoying the Birds in Your Own Backyard*. Other books have detailed advice on nature journaling, from how to draw to when to observe. The best of these is Clare Walker Leslie's *Keeping a Nature Journal*. Having a good field guide to the birds is very useful. Excellent ones have been written by David Allen Sibley, Kenn Kaufman, National Geographic, and the Audubon Society.

Clark, William S., and Brian K. Wheeler. *A Field Guide to Hawks of North America*. Houghton Mifflin Harcourt, 2001.

Dunn, Jon L., and Jonathan Alderfer. *Field Guide to the Birds of North America*. National Geographic Books, 2017.

Dunn, Jon L., and Kimball Garrett. *A Field Guide to Warblers of North America*. Houghton Mifflin Harcourt, 1997.

Kaufman, Kenn. *Kaufman Field Guide to Birds of North America*. Houghton Mifflin Harcourt, 2005.

Leslie, Clare Walker. *Keeping a Nature Journal: Deepen Your Connection with the Natural World All Around You.* Storey, 2021.

Sibley, David Allen. *The Sibley Guide to Birds,* 2nd ed. New York: Alfred A. Knopf, 2014.

Strassmann, Joan E. *Slow Birding: The Art and Science of Enjoying the Birds in Your Own Backyard.* New York: TarcherPerigee, 2022.

About the Author

Joan Strassmann is the author of *Slow Birding* and has been a slow birder all her life. She is an award-winning teacher of animal behavior, first at Rice University in Houston and then at Washington University in St. Louis, where she is the Charles Rebstock professor of biology. She has written more than two hundred scientific articles on behavior, ecology, and evolution of social organisms. She is a member of the National Academy of Sciences and the American Academy of Arts and Sciences, a fellow of the Animal Behavior Society and the American Association for the Advancement of Science, and has held a Guggenheim Fellowship. She lives with her husband in St. Louis, Missouri.